Getting at the Inner Man

Millions of Hearers
How a University Was Founded
Conwell's Splendid Efficiency
The Story of "Acres of Diamonds"

By ROBERT SHACKLETON

and

Fifty Years on the Lecture Platform

By RUSSELL H. CONWELL

CONTENTS

Millions of Hearers   1

How a University Was Founded   21

Conwell's Splendid Efficiency   39

The Story of "Acres of Diamonds"   52

Fifty Years on the Lecture Platform   64

I

MILLIONS OF HEARERS

That Conwell is not primarily a minister—that he is a minister because he is a sincere Christian, but that he is first of all an Abou Ben Adhem, a man who loves his fellow-men, becomes more and more apparent as the scope of his life-work is recognized. One almost comes to think that his pastorate of a great church is even a minor matter beside the combined importance of his educational work, his lecture work, his hospital work, his work in general as a helper to those who need help.

For my own part, I should say that he is like some of the old-time prophets, the strong ones who found a great deal to attend to in addition to matters of religion. The power, the ruggedness, the physical and mental strength, the positive grandeur of the man—all these are like the general conceptions of the big Old Testament prophets. The suggestion is given only because it has often recurred, and therefore with the feeling that there is something more than fanciful in the comparison; and yet, after all, the comparison fails in one important particular, for none of the prophets seems to have had a sense of humor!

It is perhaps better and more accurate to describe him as the last of the old school of American philosophers, the last of those sturdy-bodied, high-thinking, achieving men who, in the old days, did their best to set American humanity in the right path—such men as Emerson, Alcott, Gough, Wendell Phillips, Garrison, Bayard Taylor, Beecher;[1] men whom Conwell knew and admired in the long ago, and all of whom have long since passed away.

And Conwell, in his going up and down the country, inspiring his thousands and thousands, is the survivor of that old-time group who used to travel about, dispensing wit and wisdom and philosophy and courage to the crowded benches of country lyceums, and the chairs of school-houses and town halls, or the larger and more pretentious gathering-places of the cities.

Conwell himself is amused to remember that he wanted to talk in public from his boyhood, and that very early he began to yield to the inborn impulse. He laughs as he remembers the variety of country fairs and school commencements and anniversaries and even sewing-circles where he tried his youthful powers, and all for experience alone, in the first few years, except possibly for such a thing as a ham or a jack-knife! The first money that he ever received for speaking was, so he remembers with glee, seventy-five cents; and even that was not for his talk, but for horse hire! But at the same time there is more than amusement in recalling these experiences, for he knows that they were invaluable to him as training. And for over half a century he has affectionately remembered John B. Gough, who, in the height of his own power and success, saw resolution and possibilities in the ardent young hill-man, and actually did him the kindness and the honor of introducing him to an audience in one of the Massachusetts towns; and it was really a great kindness and a great honor, from a man who had won his fame to a young man just beginning an oratorical career.

Conwell's lecturing has been, considering everything, the most important work of his life, for by it he has come into close touch with so many millions—literally millions!—of people.

I asked him once if he had any idea how many he had talked to in the course of his career, and he tried to estimate how many thousands of times he had lectured, and the average attendance for each, but desisted when he saw that it ran into millions of hearers. What a marvel is such a fact as that! Millions of hearers!

I asked the same question of his private secretary, and found that no one had ever kept any sort of record; but as careful an estimate as could be made gave a conservative result of fully eight million hearers for his lectures; and adding the number to whom he has preached, who have been over five million, there is a total of well over thirteen million who have listened to Russell Conwell's voice! And this staggering total is, if anything, an underestimate. The figuring was done cautiously and was based upon such facts as that he now addresses an average of over forty-five hundred at his Sunday services (an average that would be higher were it not that his sermons in vacation time are usually delivered in little churches; when at home, at the Temple, he addresses three meetings every Sunday), and that he lectures throughout the entire course of each year, including six nights a week of lecturing during vacation-time. What a power is wielded by a man who has held over thirteen million people under the spell of his voice! Probably no other man who ever lived had such a total of hearers. And the total is steadily mounting, for he is a man who has never known the meaning of rest.

I think it almost certain that Dr. Conwell has never spoken to any one of what, to me, is the finest point of his lecture-work, and that is that he still goes gladly and for small fees to the small towns that are never visited by other men of great reputation. He knows that it is the little places, the out-of-the-way places, the submerged places, that most need a pleasure and a stimulus, and he still goes out, man of well over seventy that he is, to tiny towns in distant states, heedless of the discomforts of traveling, of the poor little hotels that seldom have visitors, of the oftentimes hopeless cooking and the uncleanliness, of the hardships and the discomforts, of the unventilated and overheated or underheated halls. He does not think of claiming the relaxation earned by a lifetime of labor, or, if he ever does, the thought of the sword of John Ring restores instantly his fervid earnestness.

How he does it, how he can possibly keep it up, is the greatest marvel of all. I have before me a list of his engagements for the summer weeks of this year, 1915, and I shall set it down because it will specifically show, far more clearly than general statements, the kind of work he does. The list is the itinerary of his vacation. Vacation! Lecturing every evening but Sunday, and on Sundays preaching in the town where he happens to be!

June ^{24} Ackley, Ia.

" ^{25} Waterloo, Ia.

" ^{26} Decorah, Ia.

" 27 [2]Waukon, Ia.

" 28 Red Wing, Minn.

" 29 River Ralls, Wis.

" 30 Northfield, Minn.

July 1 Faribault, Minn.

" 2 Spring Valley, Minn.

" 3 Blue Earth, Minn.

" 4 [2]Fairmount, Minn.

" 5 Lake Crystal, Minn.

" 6 Redwood Falls, Minn.

" 7 Willmer,

Minn.

" 8 Dawson,
Minn.

" 9 Redfield, S.
D.

" 10 Huron, S. D.

" 11 [2]Brookings,
S. D.

" 12 Pipestone,
Minn.

" 13 Hawarden,
Ia.

" 14 Canton, S. D.

" 15 Cherokee, Ia.

" 16 Pocahontas,
Ia.

" 17 Glidden, Ia.

" 18 [2]Boone, Ia.

" 19 Dexter, Ia.

" 20 Indianola, Ia.

" ^{21} Corydon, Ia.

" ^{22} Essex, Ia.

" ^{23} Sidney, Ia.

„   24 Falls City,
    Nebr.

„   25 [2]Hiawatha,
    Kan.

„   26 Frankfort,
    Kan.

„   27 Greenleaf,
    Kan.

„   28 Osborne,
    Kan.

„   29 Stockton,
    Kan.

„   30 Phillipsburg,
    Kan.

„   31 Mankato,
    Kan.

En route to next date on circuit.

Aug. ^{3} Westfield, Pa.

"   4 Galston, Pa.

"   5 Port Alleghany, Pa.

"   6 Wellsville, N. Y.

"   7 Bath, N. Y.

"   8 [2]Bath, N. Y.

"   9 Penn Yan, N. Y.

"   10 Athens, N. Y.

"   11 Owego, N. Y.

"   12 Patchogue, L. I., N. Y.

"   13 Port Jervis, N. Y.

"   14 Honesdale, Pa.

"   15 [2]Honesdale, Pa.

"   16 Carbondale, Pa.

"   17 Montrose, Pa.

„   18 Tunkhannock,
Pa.

„   19 Nanticoke,
Pa.

„   20 Stroudsburg,
Pa.

„   21 Newton, N. J.

„   22 [2]Newton,
N. J.

„   23 Hackettstown,
N. J.

„   24 New Hope,
Pa.

„   25 Doylestown,
Pa.

„   26 Phœnixville,
Pa.

„   27 Kennett, Pa.

„   28 Oxford, Pa.

„   29 [2]Oxford,
Pa.

And all these hardships, all this traveling and
lecturing, which would test the endurance of the

youngest and strongest, this man of over seventy assumes without receiving a particle of personal gain, for every dollar that he makes by it is given away in helping those who need helping.

That Dr. Conwell is intensely modest is one of the curious features of his character. He sincerely believes that to write his life would be, in the main, just to tell what people have done for him. He knows and admits that he works unweariedly, but in profound sincerity he ascribes the success of his plans to those who have seconded and assisted him. It is in just this way that he looks upon every phase of his life. When he is reminded of the devotion of his old soldiers, he remembers it only with a sort of pleased wonder that they gave the devotion to him, and he quite forgets that they loved him because he was always ready to sacrifice ease or risk his own life for them.

He deprecates praise; if any one likes him, the liking need not be shown in words, but in helping along a good work. That his church has succeeded has been because of the devotion of the people; that the university has succeeded is because of the splendid work of the teachers and pupils; that the hospitals have done so much has been because of the noble services of physicians and nurses. To him, as he himself expresses it, realizing that success has come to his plans, it seem as if the realities are but dreams. He is astonished by his own success. He thinks mainly of his own short-comings. "God and man have ever been very patient with me." His depression is at times profound when he compares the actual results with what he would like them to be, for always his hopes have gone soaring far in advance of achievement. It is the "Hitch your chariot to a star" idea.

His modesty goes hand-in-hand with kindliness, and I have seen him let himself be introduced in his own church to his congregation, when he is going to deliver a lecture there, just because a former pupil of the university was present who, Conwell knew, was ambitious to say something inside of the Temple walls, and this seemed to be the only opportunity.

I have noticed, when he travels, that the face of the newsboy brightens as he buys a paper from him, that the porter is all happiness, that conductor and brake-man are devotedly anxious to be of aid. Everywhere the man wins love. He loves humanity and humanity responds to the love.

He has always won the affection of those who knew him, and Bayard Taylor was one of the many; he and Bayard Taylor loved each other for long acquaintance and fellow experiences as world-wide travelers, back in the years when comparatively few Americans visited the Nile and the Orient, or even Europe.

When Taylor died there was a memorial service in Boston at which Conwell was asked to preside, and, as he wished for something more than addresses, he went to Longfellow and asked him to write and read a poem for the occasion. Longfellow had not thought of writing anything, and he was too ill to be present at the services, but, there always being something contagiously inspiring about Russell Conwell when he wishes something to be done, the poet promised to do what he could. And he wrote and sent the beautiful lines beginning:

Dead he lay among his books,
The peace of God was in his looks.

Many men of letters, including Ralph Waldo Emerson, were present at the services, and Dr. Conwell induced Oliver Wendell Holmes to read the lines, and they were listened to amid profound silence to their fine ending.

Conwell, in spite of his widespread hold on millions of people, has never won fame, recognition, general renown, compared with many men of minor achievements. This seems like an impossibility. Yet it is not an impossibility, but a fact. Great numbers of men of education and culture are entirely ignorant of him and his work in the world—men, these, who deem themselves in touch with world-affairs and with the ones who make and move the world. It is inexplicable, this, except that never was there a man more devoid of the faculty of self-exploitation, self-advertising, than Russell Conwell. Nor, in the mere reading of them, do his words appeal with anything like the force of the same words uttered by himself, for always, with his spoken words, is his personality. Those who have heard Russell Conwell, or have known him personally, recognize the charm of the man and his immense forcefulness; but there are many, and among them those who control publicity through books and newspapers, who, though they ought to be the warmest in their enthusiasm, have never felt drawn to hear him, and, if they know of him at all, think of him as one who pleases in a simple way the commoner folk, forgetting in their pride that every really great man pleases the common ones, and that simplicity and directness are attributes of real greatness.

But Russell Conwell has always won the admiration of the really great, as well as of the humbler millions. It is only a supposedly cultured class in between that is not thoroughly acquainted with what he has done.

Perhaps, too, this is owing to his having cast in his lot with the city, of all cities, which, consciously or unconsciously, looks most closely to family and place of residence as criterions of merit—a city with which it is almost impossible for a stranger to become affiliated—or aphiladelphiated, as it might be expressed—and Philadelphia, in spite of all that Dr. Conwell has done, has been under the thrall of the fact that he went north of Market Street—that fatal fact understood by all who know Philadelphia—and that he made no effort to make friends in Rittenhouse Square. Such considerations seem absurd in this twentieth century, but in Philadelphia they are still potent. Tens of thousands of Philadelphians love him, and he is honored by its greatest men, but there is a class of the pseudo-cultured who do not know him or appreciate him. And it needs also to be understood that, outside of his own beloved Temple, he would prefer to go to a little church or a little hall and to speak to the forgotten people, in the hope of encouraging and inspiring them and filling them with hopeful glow, rather than to speak to the rich and comfortable.

His dearest hope, so one of the few who are close to him told me, is that no one shall come into his life without being benefited. He does not say this publicly, nor does he for a moment believe that such a hope could be fully realized, but it is very dear to his heart; and no man spurred by such a hope, and thus bending all his thoughts toward the poor, the hard-working, the unsuccessful, is in a way to win honor from the Scribes; for we have Scribes now quite as much as when they were classed with Pharisees. It is not the first time in the world's history that Scribes have failed to give their recognition to one whose work was not among the great and wealthy.

That Conwell himself has seldom taken any part whatever in politics except as a good citizen standing for good government; that, as he expresses it, he never held any political office except that he was once on a school committee, and also that he does not identify himself with the so-called "movements" that from time to time catch public attention, but aims only and constantly at the quiet betterment of mankind, may be mentioned as additional reasons why his name and fame have not been steadily blazoned.

He knows and will admit that he works hard and has all his life worked hard. "Things keep turning my way because I'm on the job," as he whimsically expressed it one day; but that is about all, so it seems to him.

And he sincerely believes that his life has in itself been without interest; that it has been an essentially commonplace life with nothing of the interesting or the eventful to tell. He is frankly surprised that there has ever been the desire to write about him. He really has no idea of how fascinating are the things he has done. His entire life has been of positive interest from the variety of things accomplished and the unexpectedness with which he has accomplished them.

Never, for example, was there such an organizer. In fact, organization and leadership have always been as the breath of life to him. As a youth he organized debating societies and, before the war, a local military company. While on garrison duty in the Civil War he organized what is believed to have been the first free school for colored children in the South. One day Minneapolis happened to be spoken of, and Conwell happened to remember that he organized, when he was a lawyer in that city, what became the first Y. M. C. A. branch there. Once he even started a newspaper. And it was natural that the organizing instinct, as years advanced, should lead him to greater and greater things, such as his church, with the numerous associations formed within itself through his influence, and the university—the organizing of the university being in itself an achievement of positive romance.

"A life without interest!" Why, when I happened to ask, one day, how many Presidents he had known since Lincoln, he replied, quite casually, that he had "written the lives of most of them in their own homes"; and by this he meant either personally or in collaboration with the American biographer Abbott.

The many-sidedness of Conwell is one of the things that is always fascinating. After you have quite got the feeling that he is peculiarly a man of today, lecturing on today's possibilities to the people of today, you happen upon some such fact as that he attracted the attention of the London *Times* through a lecture on Italian history at Cambridge in England; or that on the evening of the day on which he was admitted to practice in the Supreme Court of the United States he gave a lecture in Washington on "The Curriculum of the Prophets in Ancient Israel." The man's life is a succession of delightful surprises.

An odd trait of his character is his love for fire. He could easily have been a veritable fire-worshiper instead of an orthodox Christian! He has always loved a blaze, and he says reminiscently that for no single thing was he punished so much when he was a child as for building bonfires. And after securing possession, as he did in middle age, of the house where he was born and of a great acreage around about, he had one of the most enjoyable times of his life in tearing down old buildings that needed to be destroyed and in heaping up fallen trees and rubbish and in piling great heaps of wood and setting the great piles ablaze. You see, there is one of the secrets of his strength—he has never lost the capacity for fiery enthusiasm!

Always, too, in these later years he is showing his strength and enthusiasm in a positively noble way. He has for years been a keen sufferer from rheumatism and neuritis, but he has never permitted this to interfere with his work or plans. He makes little of his sufferings, and when he slowly makes his way, bent and twisted, downstairs, he does not want to be noticed. "I'm all right," he will say if any one offers to help, and at such a time comes his nearest approach to impatience. He wants his suffering ignored. Strength has always been to him so precious a belonging that he will not relinquish it while he lives. "I'm all right!" And he makes himself believe that he is all right even though the pain becomes so severe as to demand massage. And he will still, even when suffering, talk calmly, or write his letters, or attend to whatever matters come before him. It is the Spartan boy hiding the pain of the gnawing fox. And he never has let pain interfere with his presence on the pulpit or the platform. He has once in a while gone to a meeting on crutches and then, by the force of will, and inspired by what he is to do, has stood before his audience or congregation, a man full of strength and fire and life.

II

HOW A UNIVERSITY WAS FOUNDED

The story of the foundation and rise of Temple University is an extraordinary story; it is not only extraordinary, but inspiring; it is not only inspiring, but full of romance.

For the university came out of nothing!— nothing but the need of a young man and the fact that he told the need to one who, throughout his life, has felt the impulse to help any one in need and has always obeyed the impulse.

I asked Dr. Conwell, up at his home in the Berkshires, to tell me himself just how the university began, and he said that it began because it was needed and succeeded because of the loyal work of the teachers. And when I asked for details he was silent for a while, looking off into the brooding twilight as it lay over the waters and the trees and the hills, and then he said:

"It was all so simple; it all came about so naturally. One evening, after a service, a young man of the congregation came to me and I saw that he was disturbed about something. I had him sit down by me, and I knew that in a few moments he would tell me what was troubling him.

"'Dr. Conwell,' he said, abruptly, 'I earn but little money, and I see no immediate chance of earning more. I have to support not only myself, but my mother. It leaves nothing at all. Yet my longing is to be a minister. It is the one ambition of my life. Is there anything that I can do?'

"'Any man,' I said to him, 'with the proper determination and ambition can study sufficiently at night to win his desire.'

"'I have tried to think so,' said he, 'but I have not been able to see anything clearly. I want to study, and am ready to give every spare minute to it, but I don't know how to get at it.'

"I thought a few minutes, as I looked at him. He was strong in his desire and in his ambition to fulfil it—strong enough, physically and mentally, for work of the body and of the mind—and he needed something more than generalizations of sympathy.

"'Come to me one evening a week and I will begin teaching you myself,' I said, 'and at least you will in that way make a beginning'; and I named the evening.

"His face brightened and he eagerly said that he would come, and left me; but in a little while he came hurrying back again. 'May I bring a friend with me?' he said.

"I told him to bring as many as he wanted to, for more than one would be an advantage, and when the evening came there were six friends with him. And that first evening I began to teach them the foundations of Latin."

He stopped as if the story was over. He was looking out thoughtfully into the waning light, and I knew that his mind was busy with those days of the beginning of the institution he so loves, and whose continued success means so much to him. In a little while he went on:

"That was the beginning of it, and there is little more to tell. By the third evening the number of pupils had increased to forty; others joined in helping me, and a room was hired; then a little house, then a second house. From a few students and teachers we became a college. After a while our buildings went up on Broad Street alongside the Temple Church, and after another while we became a university. From the first our aim"—(I noticed how quickly it had become "our" instead of "my")—"our aim was to give education to those who were unable to get it through the usual channels. And so that was really all there was to it."

That was typical of Russell Conwell—to tell with brevity of what he has done, to point out the beginnings of something, and quite omit to elaborate as to the results. And that, when you come to know him, is precisely what he means you to understand—that it is the beginning of anything that is important, and that if a thing is but earnestly begun and set going in the right way it may just as easily develop big results as little results.

But his story was very far indeed from being "all there was to it," for he had quite omitted to state the extraordinary fact that, beginning with those seven pupils, coming to his library on an evening in 1884, the Temple University has numbered, up to Commencement-time in 1915, 88,821 students! Nearly one hundred thousand students, and in the lifetime of the founder! Really, the magnitude of such a work cannot be exaggerated, nor the vast importance of it when it is considered that most of these eighty-eight thousand students would not have received their education had it not been for Temple University. And it all came from the instant response of Russell Conwell to the immediate need presented by a young man without money!

"And there is something else I want to say," said Dr. Conwell, unexpectedly. "I want to say, more fully than a mere casual word, how nobly the work was taken up by volunteer helpers; professors from the University of Pennsylvania and teachers from the public schools and other local institutions gave freely of what time they could until the new venture was firmly on its way. I honor those who came so devotedly to help. And it should be remembered that in those early days the need was even greater than it would now appear, for there were then no night schools or manual-training schools. Since then the city of Philadelphia has gone into such work, and as fast as it has taken up certain branches the Temple University has put its energy into the branches just higher. And there seems no lessening of the need of it," he added, ponderingly.

No; there is certainly no lessening of the need of it! The figures of the annual catalogue would alone show that.

As early as 1887, just three years after the beginning, the Temple College, as it was by that time called, issued its first catalogue, which set forth with stirring words that the intent of its founding was to:

"Provide such instruction as shall be best adapted to the higher education of those who are compelled to labor at their trade while engaged in study.

"Cultivate a taste for the higher and most useful branches of learning.

"Awaken in the character of young laboring men and women a determined ambition to be useful to their fellow-men."

The college—the university as it in time came to be—early broadened its scope, but it has from the first continued to aim at the needs of those unable to secure education without such help as, through its methods, it affords.

It was chartered in 1888, at which time its numbers had reached almost six hundred, and it has ever since had a constant flood of applicants. "It has demonstrated," as Dr. Conwell puts it, "that those who work for a living have time for study." And he, though he does not himself add this, has given the opportunity.

He feels especial pride in the features by which lectures and recitations are held at practically any hour which best suits the convenience of the students. If any ten students join in a request for any hour from nine in the morning to ten at night a class is arranged for them, to meet that request! This involves the necessity for a much larger number of professors and teachers than would otherwise be necessary, but that is deemed a slight consideration in comparison with the immense good done by meeting the needs of workers.

Also President Conwell—for of course he is the president of the university—is proud of the fact that the privilege of graduation depends entirely upon knowledge gained; that graduation does not depend upon having listened to any set number of lectures or upon having attended for so many terms or years. If a student can do four years' work in two years or in three he is encouraged to do it, and if he cannot even do it in four he can have no diploma.

Obviously, there is no place at Temple University for students who care only for a few years of leisured ease. It is a place for workers, and not at all for those who merely wish to be able to boast that they attended a university. The students have come largely from among railroad clerks, bank clerks, bookkeepers, teachers, preachers, mechanics, salesmen, drug clerks, city and United States government employees, widows, nurses, housekeepers, brakemen, firemen, engineers, motormen, conductors, and shop hands.

It was when the college became strong enough, and sufficiently advanced in scholarship and standing, and broad enough in scope, to win the name of university that this title was officially granted to it by the State of Pennsylvania, in 1907, and now its educational plan includes three distinct school systems.

First: it offers a high-school education to the student who has to quit school after leaving the grammar-school.

Second: it offers a full college education, with the branches taught in long-established high-grade colleges, to the student who has to quit on leaving the high-school.

Third: it offers further scientific or professional education to the college graduate who must go to work immediately on quitting college, but who wishes to take up some such course as law or medicine or engineering.

Out of last year's enrolment of 3,654 it is interesting to notice that the law claimed 141; theology, 182; medicine and pharmacy and dentistry combined, 357; civil engineering, 37; also that the teachers' college, with normal courses on such subjects as household arts and science, kindergarten work, and physical education, took 174; and still more interesting, in a way, to see that 269 students were enrolled for the technical and vocational courses, such as cooking and dress-making, millinery, manual crafts, school-gardening, and story-telling. There were 511 in high-school work, and 243 in elementary education. There were 79 studying music, and 68 studying to be trained nurses. There were 606 in the college of liberal arts and sciences, and in the department of commercial education there were 987—for it is a university that offers both scholarship and practicality.

Temple University is not in the least a charitable institution. Its fees are low, and its hours are for the convenience of the students themselves, but it is a place of absolute independence. It is, indeed, a place of far greater independence, so one of the professors pointed out, than are the great universities which receive millions and millions of money in private gifts and endowments.

Temple University in its early years was sorely in need of money, and often there were thrills of expectancy when some man of mighty wealth seemed on the point of giving. But not a single one ever did, and now the Temple likes to feel that it is glad of it. The Temple, to quote its own words, is "An institution for strong men and women who can labor with both mind and body."

And the management is proud to be able to say that, although great numbers have come from distant places, "not one of the many thousands ever failed to find an opportunity to support himself."

Even in the early days, when money was needed for the necessary buildings (the buildings of which Conwell dreamed when he left second-story doors in his church!), the university—college it was then called—had won devotion from those who knew that it was a place where neither time nor money was wasted, and where idleness was a crime, and in the donations for the work were many such items as four hundred dollars from factory-workers who gave fifty cents each, and two thousand dollars from policemen who gave a dollar each. Within two or three years past the State of Pennsylvania has begun giving it a large sum annually, and this state aid is public recognition of Temple University as an institution of high public value. The state money is invested in the brains and hearts of the ambitious.

So eager is Dr. Conwell to place the opportunity of education before every one, that even his servants must go to school! He is not one of those who can see needs that are far away but not those that are right at home. His belief in education, and in the highest attainable education, is profound, and it is not only on account of the abstract pleasure and value of education, but its power of increasing actual earning power and thus making a worker of more value to both himself and the community.

Many a man and many a woman, while continuing to work for some firm or factory, has taken Temple technical courses and thus fitted himself or herself for an advanced position with the same employer. The Temple knows of many such, who have thus won prominent advancement. And it knows of teachers who, while continuing to teach, have fitted themselves through the Temple courses for professorships. And it knows of many a case of the rise of a Temple student that reads like an Arabian Nights' fancy!—of advance from bookkeeper to editor, from office-boy to bank president, from kitchen maid to school principal, from street-cleaner to mayor! The Temple University helps them that help themselves.

President Conwell told me personally of one case that especially interested him because it seemed to exhibit, in especial degree, the Temple possibilities; and it particularly interested me because it also showed, in high degree, the methods and personality of Dr. Conwell himself.

One day a young woman came to him and said she earned only three dollars a week and that she desired very much to make more. "Can you tell me how to do it?" she said.

He liked her ambition and her directness, but there was something that he felt doubtful about, and that was that her hat looked too expensive for three dollars a week!

Now Dr. Conwell is a man whom you would never suspect of giving a thought to the hat of man or woman! But as a matter of fact there is very little that he does not see.

But though the hat seemed too expensive for three dollars a week, Dr. Conwell is not a man who makes snap-judgments harshly, and in particular he would be the last man to turn away hastily one who had sought him out for help. He never felt, nor could possibly urge upon any one, contentment with a humble lot; he stands for advancement; he has no sympathy with that dictum of the smug, that has come to us from a nation tight bound for centuries by its gentry and aristocracy, about being contented with the position in which God has placed you, for he points out that the Bible itself holds up advancement and success as things desirable.

And, as to the young woman before him, it developed, through discreet inquiry veiled by frank discussion of her case, that she had made the expensive-looking hat herself! Whereupon not only did all doubtfulness and hesitation vanish, but he saw at once how she could better herself. He knew that a woman who could make a hat like that for herself could make hats for other people, and so, "Go into millinery as a business," he advised.

"Oh—if I only could!" she exclaimed. "But I know that I don't know enough."

"Take the millinery course in Temple University," he responded.

She had not even heard of such a course, and when he went on to explain how she could take it and at the same time continue at her present work until the course was concluded, she was positively ecstatic—it was all so unexpected, this opening of the view of a new and broader life.

"She was an unusual woman," concluded Dr. Conwell, "and she worked with enthusiasm and tirelessness. She graduated, went to an up-state city that seemed to offer a good field, opened a millinery establishment there, with her own name above the door, and became prosperous. That was only a few years ago. And recently I had a letter from her, telling me that last year she netted a clear profit of three thousand six hundred dollars!"

I remember a man, himself of distinguished position, saying of Dr. Conwell, "It is difficult to speak in tempered language of what he has achieved." And that just expresses it; the temptation is constantly to use superlatives— for superlatives fit! Of course he has succeeded for himself, and succeeded marvelously, in his rise from the rocky hill farm, but he has done so vastly more than that in inspiring such hosts of others to succeed!

A dreamer of dreams and a seer of visions— and what realizations have come! And it interested me profoundly not long ago, when Dr. Conwell, talking of the university, unexpectedly remarked that he would like to see such institutions scattered throughout every state in the Union. "All carried on at slight expense to the students and at hours to suit all sorts of working men and women," he added, after a pause; and then, abruptly, "I should like to see the possibility of higher education offered to every one in the United States who works for a living."

There was something superb in the very imagining of such a nation-wide system. But I did not ask whether or not he had planned any details for such an effort. I knew that thus far it might only be one of his dreams—but I also knew that his dreams had a way of becoming realities. I had a fleeting glimpse of his soaring vision. It was amazing to find a man of more than three-score and ten thus dreaming of more worlds to conquer. And I thought, what could the world have accomplished if Methuselah had been a Conwell!—or, far better, what wonders could be accomplished if Conwell could but be a Methuselah!

He has all his life been a great traveler. He is a man who sees vividly and who can describe vividly. Yet often his letters, even from places of the most profound interest, are mostly concerned with affairs back home. It is not that he does not feel, and feel intensely, the interest of what he is visiting, but that his tremendous earnestness keeps him always concerned about his work at home. There could be no stronger example than what I noticed in a letter he wrote from Jerusalem. "I am in Jerusalem! And here

at Gethsemane and at the Tomb of Christ"—
reading thus far, one expects that any man, and
especially a minister, is sure to say something
regarding the associations of the place and the
effect of these associations on his mind; but
Conwell is always the man who is different—
"And here at Gethsemane and at the Tomb of
Christ, I pray especially for the Temple
University." That is Conwellism!

That he founded a hospital—a work in itself
great enough for even a great life—is but one
among the striking incidents of his career. And
it came about through perfect naturalness. For
he came to know, through his pastoral work and
through his growing acquaintance with the
needs of the city, that there was a vast amount
of suffering and wretchedness and anguish,
because of the inability of the existing hospitals
to care for all who needed care. There was so
much sickness and suffering to be alleviated,
there were so many deaths that could be
prevented—and so he decided to start another
hospital.

And, like everything with him, the beginning
was small. That cannot too strongly be set down
as the way of this phenomenally successful
organizer. Most men would have to wait until a
big beginning could be made, and so would
most likely never make a beginning at all. But

Conwell's way is to dream of future bigness, but be ready to begin at once, no matter how small or insignificant the beginning may appear to others.

Two rented rooms, one nurse, one patient—this was the humble beginning, in 1891, of what has developed into the great Samaritan Hospital. In a year there was an entire house, fitted up with wards and operating-room. Now it occupies several buildings, including and adjoining that first one, and a great new structure is planned. But even as it is, it has a hundred and seventy beds, is fitted with all modern hospital appliances, and has a large staff of physicians; and the number of surgical operations performed there is very large.

It is open to sufferers of any race or creed, and the poor are never refused admission, the rule being that treatment is free for those who cannot pay, but that such as can afford it shall pay according to their means.

And the hospital has a kindly feature that endears it to patients and their relatives alike, and that is that, by Dr. Conwell's personal order, there are not only the usual week-day hours for visiting, but also one evening a week and every Sunday afternoon. "For otherwise," as he says, "many would be unable to come because they could not get away from their work."

A little over eight years ago another hospital was taken in charge, the Garretson—not founded by Conwell, this one, but acquired, and promptly expanded in its usefulness.

Both the Samaritan and the Garretson are part of Temple University. The Samaritan Hospital has treated, since its foundation, up to the middle of 1915, 29,301 patients; the Garretson, in its shorter life, 5,923. Including dispensary cases as well as house patients, the two hospitals together, under the headship of President Conwell, have handled over 400,000 cases.

How Conwell can possibly meet the multifarious demands upon his time is in itself a miracle. He is the head of the great church; he is the head of the university; he is the head of the hospitals; he is the head of everything with which he is associated! And he is not only nominally, but very actively, the head!

III

HIS SPLENDID EFFICIENCY

Conwell has a few strong and efficient executive helpers who have long been associated with him; men and women who know his ideas and ideals, who are devoted to him, and who do their utmost to relieve him; and of course there is very much that is thus done for him; but even as it is, he is so overshadowing a man (there is really no other word) that all who work with him look to him for advice and guidance—the professors and the students, the doctors and the nurses, the church officers, the Sunday-school teachers, the members of his congregation. And he is never too busy to see any one who really wishes to see him.

He can attend to a vast intricacy of detail, and answer myriad personal questions and doubts, and keep the great institutions splendidly going, by thorough systematization of time, and by watching every minute. He has several secretaries, for special work, besides his private secretary. His correspondence is very great. Often he dictates to a secretary as he travels on the train. Even in the few days for which he can run back to the Berkshires, work is awaiting him. Work follows him. And after knowing of this, one is positively amazed that he is able to give to his country-wide lectures the time and the traveling that they inexorably demand. Only a man of immense strength, of the greatest stamina, a veritable superman, could possibly do it. And at times one quite forgets, noticing the multiplicity of his occupations, that he prepares two sermons and two talks on Sunday!

Here is his usual Sunday schedule, when at home. He rises at seven and studies until breakfast, which is at eight-thirty. Then he studies until nine-forty-five, when he leads a men's meeting at which he is likely also to play the organ and lead the singing. At ten-thirty is the principal church service, at which he preaches, and at the close of which he shakes hands with hundreds. He dines at one, after which he takes fifteen minutes' rest and then reads; and at three o'clock he addresses, in a talk that is like another sermon, a large class of men—not the same men as in the morning. He is also sure to look in at the regular session of the Sunday-school. Home again, where he studies and reads until supper-time. At seven-thirty is the evening service, at which he again preaches and after which he shakes hands with several hundred more and talks personally, in his study, with any who have need of talk with him. He is usually home by ten-thirty. I spoke of it, one evening, as having been a strenuous day, and he responded, with a cheerfully whimsical smile: "Three sermons and shook hands with nine hundred."

That evening, as the service closed, he had said to the congregation: "I shall be here for an hour. We always have a pleasant time together after service. If you are acquainted with me, come up and shake hands. If you are strangers"—just the slightest of pauses—"come up and let us make an acquaintance that will last for eternity." I remember how simply and easily this was said, in his clear, deep voice, and how impressive and important it seemed, and with what unexpectedness it came. "Come and make an acquaintance that will last for eternity!" And there was a serenity about his way of saying this which would make strangers think—just as he meant them to think—that he had nothing whatever to do but to talk with them. Even his own congregation have, most of them, little conception of how busy a man he is and how precious is his time.

One evening last June—to take an evening of which I happened to know—he got home from a journey of two hundred miles at six o'clock, and after dinner and a slight rest went to the church prayer-meeting, which he led in his usual vigorous way at such meetings, playing the organ and leading the singing, as well as praying and talking. After the prayer-meeting he went to two dinners in succession, both of them important dinners in connection with the close of the university year, and at both dinners he spoke. At the second dinner he was notified of the sudden illness of a member of his congregation, and instantly hurried to the man's home and thence to the hospital to which he had been removed, and there he remained at the man's bedside, or in consultation with the physicians, until one in the morning. Next morning he was up at seven and again at work.

"This one thing I do," is his private maxim of efficiency, and a literalist might point out that he does not one thing only, but a thousand things, not getting Conwell's meaning, which is that whatever the thing may be which he is doing he lets himself think of nothing else until it is done.

Dr. Conwell has a profound love for the country and particularly for the country of his own youth. He loves the wind that comes sweeping over the hills, he loves the wide-stretching views from the heights and the forest intimacies of the nestled nooks. He loves the rippling streams, he loves the wild flowers that nestle in seclusion or that unexpectedly paint some mountain meadow with delight. He loves the very touch of the earth, and he loves the great bare rocks.

He writes verses at times; at least he has written lines for a few old tunes; and it interested me greatly to chance upon some lines of his that picture heaven in terms of the Berkshires:

The wide-stretching valleys in colors so fadeless,
Where trees are all deathless and flowers e'er bloom.

That is heaven in the eyes of a New England hill-man! Not golden pavement and ivory palaces, but valleys and trees and flowers and the wide sweep of the open.

Few things please him more than to go, for example, blackberrying, and he has a knack of never scratching his face or his fingers when doing so. And he finds blackberrying, whether he goes alone or with friends, an extraordinarily good time for planning something he wishes to do or working out the thought of a sermon. And fishing is even better, for in fishing he finds immense recreation and restfulness and at the same time a further opportunity to think and plan.

As a small boy he wished that he could throw a dam across the trout-brook that runs near the little Conwell home, and—as he never gives up—he finally realized the ambition, although it was after half a century! And now he has a big pond, three-quarters of a mile long by half a mile wide, lying in front of the house, down a slope from it—a pond stocked with splendid pickerel. He likes to float about restfully on this pond, thinking or fishing, or both. And on that pond he showed me how to catch pickerel even under a blaze of sunlight!

He is a trout-fisher, too, for it is a trout stream that feeds this pond and goes dashing away from it through the wilderness; and for miles adjoining his place a fishing club of wealthy men bought up the rights in this trout stream, and they approached him with a liberal offer. But he declined it. "I remembered what good times I had when I was a boy, fishing up and down that stream, and I couldn't think of keeping the boys of the present day from such a pleasure. So they may still come and fish for trout here."

As we walked one day beside this brook, he suddenly said: "Did you ever notice that every brook has its own song? I should know the song of this brook anywhere."

It would seem as if he loved his rugged native country because it is rugged even more than because it is native! Himself so rugged, so hardy, so enduring—the strength of the hills is his also.

Always, in his very appearance, you see something of this ruggedness of the hills; a ruggedness, a sincerity, a plainness, that mark alike his character and his looks. And always one realizes the strength of the man, even when his voice, as it usually is, is low. And one increasingly realizes the strength when, on the lecture platform or in the pulpit or in conversation, he flashes vividly into fire.

A big-boned man he is, sturdy-framed, a tall man, with broad shoulders and strong hands. His hair is a deep chestnut-brown that at first sight seems black. In his early manhood he was superb in looks, as his pictures show, but anxiety and work and the constant flight of years, with physical pain, have settled his face into lines of sadness and almost of severity, which instantly vanish when he speaks. And his face is illumined by marvelous eyes.

He is a lonely man. The wife of his early years died long, long ago, before success had come, and she was deeply mourned, for she had loyally helped him through a time that held much of struggle and hardship. He married again; and this wife was his loyal helpmate for many years. In a time of special stress, when a defalcation of sixty-five thousand dollars threatened to crush Temple College just when it was getting on its feet, for both Temple Church and Temple College had in those early days buoyantly assumed heavy indebtedness, he raised every dollar he could by selling or mortgaging his own possessions, and in this his wife, as he lovingly remembers, most cordially stood beside him, although she knew that if anything should happen to him the financial sacrifice would leave her penniless. She died after years of companionship; his children married and made homes of their own; he is a lonely man. Yet he is not unhappy, for the tremendous demands of his tremendous work leave him little time for sadness or retrospect. At times the realization comes that he is getting old, that friends and comrades have been passing away, leaving him an old man with younger friends and helpers. But such realization only makes him work with an earnestness still more intense, knowing that the night cometh when no man shall work.

Deeply religious though he is, he does not force religion into conversation on ordinary subjects or upon people who may not be interested in it.

With him, it is action and good works, with faith and belief, that count, except when talk is the natural, the fitting, the necessary thing; when addressing either one individual or thousands, he talks with superb effectiveness.

His sermons are, it may almost literally be said, parable after parable; although he himself would be the last man to say this, for it would sound as if he claimed to model after the greatest of all examples. His own way of putting it is that he uses stories frequently because people are more impressed by illustrations than by argument.

Always, whether in the pulpit or out of it, he is simple and homelike, human and unaffected. If he happens to see some one in the congregation to whom he wishes to speak, he may just leave his pulpit and walk down the aisle, while the choir is singing, and quietly say a few words and return.

In the early days of his ministry, if he heard of a poor family in immediate need of food he would be quite likely to gather a basket of provisions and go personally, and offer this assistance and such other as he might find necessary when he reached the place. As he became known he ceased from this direct and open method of charity, for he knew that impulsiveness would be taken for intentional display. But he has never ceased to be ready to help on the instant that he knows help is needed. Delay and lengthy investigation are avoided by him when he can be certain that something immediate is required. And the extent of his quiet charity is amazing. With no family for which to save money, and with no care to put away money for himself, he thinks only of money as an instrument for helpfulness. I never heard a friend criticize him except for too great open-handedness.

I was strongly impressed, after coming to know him, that he possessed many of the qualities that made for the success of the old-time district leaders of New York City, and I mentioned this to him, and he at once responded that he had himself met "Big Tim," the long-time leader of the Sullivans, and had had him at his house, Big Tim having gone to Philadelphia to aid some henchman in trouble, and having promptly sought the aid of Dr. Conwell. And it was characteristic of Conwell that he saw, what so many never saw, the most striking characteristic of that Tammany leader. For, "Big Tim Sullivan was so kind-hearted!" Conwell appreciated the man's political unscrupulousness as well as did his enemies, but he saw also what made his underlying   power—his   kind-heartedness.

Except that Sullivan could be supremely unscrupulous, and that Conwell is supremely scrupulous, there were marked similarities in these masters over men; and Conwell possesses, as Sullivan possessed, a wonderful memory for faces and names.

Naturally, Russell Conwell stands steadily and strongly for good citizenship. But he never talks boastful Americanism. He seldom speaks in so many words of either Americanism or good citizenship, but he constantly and silently keeps the American flag, as the symbol of good citizenship, before his people. An American flag is prominent in his church; an American flag is seen in his home; a beautiful American flag is up at his Berkshire place and surmounts a lofty tower where, when he was a boy, there stood a mighty tree at the top of which was an eagle's nest, which has given him a name for his home, for he terms it "The Eagle's Nest."

Remembering a long story that I had read of his climbing to the top of that tree, though it was a well-nigh impossible feat, and securing the nest by great perseverance and daring, I asked him if the story were a true one. "Oh, I've heard something about it; somebody said that somebody watched me, or something of the kind. But I don't remember anything about it myself."

Any friend of his is sure to say something, after a while, about his determination, his insistence on going ahead with anything on which he has really set his heart. One of the very important things on which he insisted, in spite of very great opposition, and especially an opposition from the other churches of his denomination (for this was a good many years ago, when there was much more narrowness in churches and sects than there is at present), was with regard to doing away with close communion. He determined on an open communion; and his way of putting it, once decided upon, was: "My friends, it is not for me to invite you to the table of the Lord. The table of the Lord is open. If you feel that you can come to the table, it is open to you." And this is the form which he still uses.

He not only never gives up, but, so his friends say, he never forgets a thing upon which he has once decided, and at times, long after they supposed the matter has been entirely forgotten, they suddenly find Dr. Conwell bringing his original purpose to pass. When I was told of this I remembered that pickerel-pond in the Berkshires!

If he is really set upon doing anything, little or big, adverse criticism does not disturb his serenity. Some years ago he began wearing a huge diamond, whose size attracted much criticism and caustic comment. He never said a word in defense; he just kept on wearing the diamond. One day, however, after some years, he took it off, and people said, "He has listened to the criticism at last!" He smiled reminiscently as he told me about this, and said: "A dear old deacon of my congregation gave me that diamond and I did not like to hurt his feelings by refusing it. It really bothered me to wear such a glaring big thing, but because I didn't want to hurt the old deacon's feelings I kept on wearing it until he was dead. Then I stopped wearing it."

The ambition of Russell Conwell is to continue working and working until the very last moment of his life. In work he forgets his sadness, his loneliness, his age. And he said to me one day, "I will die in harness."

IV

THE STORY OF "ACRES OF DIAMONDS"

Considering everything, the most remarkable thing in Russell Conwell's remarkable life is his lecture, "Acres of Diamonds." That is, the lecture itself, the number of times he has delivered it, what a source of inspiration it has been to myriads, the money that he has made and is making, and, still more, the purpose to which he directs the money. In the circumstances surrounding "Acres of Diamonds," in its tremendous success, in the attitude of mind revealed by the lecture itself and by what Dr. Conwell does with it, it is illuminative of his character, his aims, his ability.

The lecture is vibrant with his energy. It flashes with his hopefulness. It is full of his enthusiasm. It is packed full of his intensity. It stands for the possibilities of success in every one. He has delivered it over five thousand times. The demand for it never diminishes. The success grows never less.

There is a time in Russell Conwell's youth of which it is pain for him to think. He told me of it one evening, and his voice sank lower and lower as he went far back into the past. It was of his days at Yale that he spoke, for they were days of suffering. For he had not money for Yale, and in working for more he endured bitter humiliation. It was not that the work was hard, for Russell Conwell has always been ready for hard work. It was not that there were privations and difficulties, for he has always found difficulties only things to overcome, and endured privations with cheerful fortitude. But it was the humiliations that he met—the personal humiliations that after more than half a century make him suffer in remembering them—yet out of those humiliations came a marvelous result.

"I determined," he says, "that whatever I could do to make the way easier at college for other young men working their way I would do."

And so, many years ago, he began to devote every dollar that he made from "Acres of Diamonds" to this definite purpose. He has what may be termed a waiting-list. On that list are very few cases he has looked into personally. Infinitely busy man that he is, he cannot do extensive personal investigation. A large proportion of his names come to him from college presidents who know of students in their own colleges in need of such a helping hand.

"Every night," he said, when I asked him to tell me about it, "when my lecture is over and the check is in my hand, I sit down in my room in the hotel"—what a lonely picture, too!—"I sit down in my room in the hotel and subtract from the total sum received my actual expenses for that place, and make out a check for the difference and send it to some young man on my list. And I always send with the check a letter of advice and helpfulness, expressing my hope that it will be of some service to him and telling him that he is to feel under no obligation except to his Lord. I feel strongly, and I try to make every young man feel, that there must be no sense of obligation to me personally. And I tell them that I am hoping to leave behind me men who will do more work than I have done. Don't think that I put in too much advice," he added, with a smile, "for I only try to let them know that a friend is trying to help them."

His face lighted as he spoke. "There is such a fascination in it!" he exclaimed. "It is just like a gamble! And as soon as I have sent the letter and crossed a name off my list, I am aiming for the next one!"

And after a pause he added: "I do not attempt to send any young man enough for all his expenses. But I want to save him from bitterness, and each check will help. And, too," he concluded, naïvely, in the vernacular, "I don't want them to lay down on me!"

He told me that he made it clear that he did not wish to get returns or reports from this branch of his life-work, for it would take a great deal of time in watching and thinking and in the reading and writing of letters. "But it is mainly," he went on, "that I do not wish to hold over their heads the sense of obligation."

When I suggested that this was surely an example of bread cast upon the waters that could not return, he was silent for a little and then said, thoughtfully: "As one gets on in years there is satisfaction in doing a thing for the sake of doing it. The bread returns in the sense of effort made."

On a recent trip through Minnesota he was positively upset, so his secretary told me, through being recognized on a train by a young man who had been helped through "Acres of Diamonds," and who, finding that this was really Dr. Conwell, eagerly brought his wife to join him in most fervent thanks for his assistance. Both the husband and his wife were so emotionally overcome that it quite overcame Dr. Conwell himself.

The lecture, to quote the noble words of Dr. Conwell himself, is designed to help "every person, of either sex, who cherishes the high resolve of sustaining a career of usefulness and honor." It is a lecture of helpfulness. And it is a lecture, when given with Conwell's voice and face and manner, that is full of fascination. And yet it is all so simple!

It is packed full of inspiration, of suggestion, of aid. He alters it to meet the local circumstances of the thousands of different places in which he delivers it. But the base remains the same. And even those to whom it is an old story will go to hear him time after time. It amuses him to say that he knows individuals who have listened to it twenty times.

It begins with a story told to Conwell by an old Arab as the two journeyed together toward Nineveh, and, as you listen, you hear the actual voices and you see the sands of the desert and the waving palms. The lecturer's voice is so easy, so effortless, it seems so ordinary and matter-of-fact—yet the entire scene is instantly vital and alive! Instantly the man has his audience under a sort of spell, eager to listen, ready to be merry or grave. He has the faculty of control, the vital quality that makes the orator.

The same people will go to hear this lecture over and over, and that is the kind of tribute that Conwell likes. I recently heard him deliver it in his own church, where it would naturally be thought to be an old story, and where, presumably, only a few of the faithful would go; but it was quite clear that all of his church are the faithful, for it was a large audience that came to listen to him; hardly a seat in the great auditorium was vacant. And it should be added that, although it was in his own church, it was not a free lecture, where a throng might be expected, but that each one paid a liberal sum for a seat—and the paying of admission is always a practical test of the sincerity of desire to hear. And the people were swept along by the current as if lecturer and lecture were of novel interest. The lecture in itself is good to read, but it is only when it is illumined by Conwell's vivid personality that one understands how it influences in the actual delivery.

On that particular evening he had decided to give the lecture in the same form as when he first delivered it many years ago, without any of the alterations that have come with time and changing localities, and as he went on, with the audience rippling and bubbling with laughter as usual, he never doubted that he was giving it as he had given it years before; and yet—so up-to-date and alive must he necessarily be, in spite of a definitive effort to set himself back—every once in a while he was coming out with illustrations from such distinctly recent things as the automobile!

The last time I heard him was the 5,124th time for the lecture. Doesn't it seem incredible! 5,124 times! I noticed that he was to deliver it at a little out-of-the-way place, difficult for any considerable number to get to, and I wondered just how much of an audience would gather and how they would be impressed. So I went over from where I was, a few miles away. The road was dark and I pictured a small audience, but when I got there I found the church building in which he was to deliver the lecture had a seating capacity of 830 and that precisely 830 people were already seated there and that a fringe of others were standing behind. Many had come from miles away. Yet the lecture had scarcely, if at all, been advertised. But people had said to one another: "Aren't you going to hear Dr. Conwell?" And the word had thus been passed along.

I remember how fascinating it was to watch that audience, for they responded so keenly and with such heartfelt pleasure throughout the entire lecture. And not only were they immensely pleased and amused and interested—and to achieve that at a crossroads church was in itself a triumph to be proud of—but I knew that every listener was given an impulse toward doing something for himself and for others, and that with at least some of them the impulse would materialize in acts. Over and over one realizes what a power such a man wields.

And what an unselfishness! For, far on in years as he is, and suffering pain, he does not chop down his lecture to a definite length; he does not talk for just an hour or go on grudgingly for an hour and a half. He sees that the people are fascinated and inspired, and he forgets pain, ignores time, forgets that the night is late and that he has a long journey to go to get home, and keeps on generously for two hours! And every one wishes it were four.

Always he talks with ease and sympathy. There are geniality, composure, humor, simple and homely jests—yet never does the audience forget that he is every moment in tremendous earnest. They bubble with responsive laughter or are silent in riveted attention. A stir can be seen to sweep over an audience, of earnestness or surprise or amusement or resolve. When he is grave and sober or fervid the people feel that he is himself a fervidly earnest man, and when he is telling something humorous there is on his part almost a repressed chuckle, a genial appreciation of the fun of it, not in the least as if he were laughing at his own humor, but as if he and his hearers were laughing together at something of which they were all humorously cognizant.

Myriad successes in life have come through the direct inspiration of this single lecture. One hears of so many that there must be vastly more that are never told. A few of the most recent were told me by Dr. Conwell himself, one being of a farmer boy who walked a long distance to hear him. On his way home, so the boy, now a man, has written him, he thought over and over of what he could do to advance himself, and before he reached home he learned that a teacher was wanted at a certain country school. He knew he did not know enough to teach, but was sure he could learn, so he bravely asked for the place. And something in his earnestness made him win a temporary appointment. Thereupon he worked and studied so hard and so devotedly, while he daily taught, that within a few months he was regularly employed there. "And now," says Conwell, abruptly, with his characteristic skimming over of the intermediate details between the important beginning of a thing and the satisfactory end, "and now that young man is one of our college presidents."

And very recently a lady came to Dr. Conwell, the wife of an exceptionally prominent man who was earning a large salary, and she told him that her husband was so unselfishly generous with money that often they were almost in straits. And she said they had bought a little farm as a country place, paying only a few hundred dollars for it, and that she had said to herself, laughingly, after hearing the lecture, "There are no acres of diamonds on this place!" But she also went on to tell that she had found a spring of exceptionally fine water there, although in buying they had scarcely known of the spring at all; and she had been so inspired by Conwell that she had had the water analyzed and, finding that it was remarkably pure, had begun to have it bottled and sold under a trade name as special spring water. And she is making money. And she also sells pure ice from the pool, cut in winter-time—and all because of "Acres of Diamonds"!

Several millions of dollars, in all, have been received by Russell Conwell as the proceeds from this single lecture. Such a fact is almost staggering—and it is more staggering to realize what good is done in the world by this man, who does not earn for himself, but uses his money in immediate helpfulness. And one can neither think nor write with moderation when it is further realized that far more good than can be done directly with money he does by uplifting and inspiring with this lecture. Always his heart is with the weary and the heavy-laden. Always he stands for self-betterment.

Last year, 1914, he and his work were given unique recognition. For it was known by his friends that this particular lecture was approaching its five-thousandth delivery, and they planned a celebration of such an event in the history of the most popular lecture in the world. Dr. Conwell agreed to deliver it in the Academy of Music, in Philadelphia, and the building was packed and the streets outside were thronged. The proceeds from all sources for that five-thousandth lecture were over nine thousand dollars.

The hold which Russell Conwell has gained on the affections and respect of his home city was seen not only in the thousands who strove to hear him, but in the prominent men who served on the local committee in charge of the celebration. There was a national committee, too, and the nation-wide love that he has won, the nation-wide appreciation of what he has done and is still doing, was shown by the fact that among the names of the notables on this committee were those of nine governors of states. The Governor of Pennsylvania was himself present to do Russell Conwell honor, and he gave to him a key emblematic of the Freedom of the State.

The "Freedom of the State"—yes; this man, well over seventy, has won it. The Freedom of the State, the Freedom of the Nation—for this man of helpfulness, this marvelous exponent of the gospel of success, has worked marvelously for the freedom, the betterment, the liberation, the advancement, of the individual.

FIFTY YEARS ON THE LECTURE PLATFORM

BY Russell H. Conwell

An autobiography! What an absurd request! If all the conditions were favorable, the story of my public life could not be made interesting. It does not seem possible that any will care to read so plain and uneventful a tale. I see nothing in it for boasting, nor much that could be helpful. Then I never saved a scrap of paper intentionally concerning my work to which I could refer, not a book, not a sermon, not a lecture, not a newspaper notice or account, not a magazine article, not one of the kind biographies written from time to time by noble friends have I ever kept even as a souvenir, although some of them may be in my library. I have ever felt that the writers concerning my life were too generous and that my own work was too hastily done. Hence I have nothing upon which to base an autobiographical account, except the recollections which come to an overburdened mind.

My general view of half a century on the lecture platform brings to me precious and beautiful memories, and fills my soul with devout gratitude for the blessings and kindnesses which have been given to me so far beyond my deserts. So much more success has come to my hands than I ever expected; so much more of good have I found than even youth's wildest dream included; so much more effective have been my weakest endeavors than I ever planned or hoped—that a biography written truthfully would be mostly an account of what men and women have done for me.

I have lived to see accomplished far more than my highest ambition included, and have seen the enterprises I have undertaken rush by me, pushed on by a thousand strong hands until they have left me far behind them. The realities are like dreams to me. Blessings on the loving hearts and noble minds who have been so willing to sacrifice for others' good and to think only of what they could do, and never of what they should get! Many of them have ascended into the Shining Land, and here I am in mine age gazing up alone,

Only waiting till the shadows
Are a little longer grown.

Fifty years! I was a young man, not yet of age, when I delivered my first platform lecture. The Civil War of 1861-65 drew on with all its passions, patriotism, horrors, and fears, and I was studying law at Yale University. I had from childhood felt that I was "called to the ministry." The earliest event of memory is the prayer of my father at family prayers in the little old cottage in the Hampshire highlands of the Berkshire Hills, calling on God with a sobbing voice to lead me into some special service for the Saviour. It filled me with awe, dread, and fear, and I recoiled from the thought, until I determined to fight against it with all my power. So I sought for other professions and for decent excuses for being anything but a preacher.

Yet while I was nervous and timid before the class in declamation and dreaded to face any kind of an audience, I felt in my soul a strange impulsion toward public speaking which for years made me miserable. The war and the public meetings for recruiting soldiers furnished an outlet for my suppressed sense of duty, and my first lecture was on the "Lessons of History" as applied to the campaigns against the Confederacy.

That matchless temperance orator and loving friend, John B. Gough, introduced me to the little audience in Westfield, Massachusetts, in 1862. What a foolish little school-boy speech it must have been! But Mr. Gough's kind words of praise, the bouquets and the applause, made me feel that somehow the way to public oratory would not be so hard as I had feared.

From that time I acted on Mr. Gough's advice and "sought practice" by accepting almost every invitation I received to speak on any kind of a subject. There were many sad failures and tears, but it was a restful compromise with my conscience concerning the ministry, and it pleased my friends. I addressed picnics, Sunday-schools, patriotic meetings, funerals, anniversaries, commencements, debates, cattle-shows, and sewing-circles without partiality and without price. For the first five years the income was all experience. Then voluntary gifts began to come occasionally in the shape of a jack-knife, a ham, a book, and the first cash remuneration was from a farmers' club, of seventy-five cents toward the "horse hire." It was a curious fact that one member of that club afterward moved to Salt Lake City and was a member of the committee at the Mormon Tabernacle in 1872 which, when I was a correspondent, on a journey around the world, employed me to lecture on "Men of the Mountains" in the Mormon Tabernacle, at a fee of five hundred dollars.

While I was gaining practice in the first years of platform work, I had the good fortune to have profitable employment as a soldier, or as a correspondent or lawyer, or as an editor or as a preacher, which enabled me to pay my own expenses, and it has been seldom in the fifty years that I have ever taken a fee for my personal use. In the last thirty-six years I have dedicated solemnly all the lecture income to benevolent enterprises. If I am antiquated enough for an autobiography, perhaps I may be aged enough to avoid the criticism of being an egotist, when I state that some years I delivered one lecture, "Acres of Diamonds," over two hundred times each year, at an average income of about one hundred and fifty dollars for each lecture.

It was a remarkable good fortune which came to me as a lecturer when Mr. James Redpath organized the first lecture bureau ever established. Mr. Redpath was the biographer of John Brown of Harper's Ferry renown, and as Mr. Brown had been long a friend of my father's I found employment, while a student on vacation, in selling that life of John Brown. That acquaintance with Mr. Redpath was maintained until Mr. Redpath's death. To General Charles H. Taylor, with whom I was employed for a time as reporter for the Boston *Daily Traveler*, I was indebted for many acts of self-sacrificing friendship which soften my soul as I recall them. He did me the greatest kindness when he suggested my name to Mr. Redpath as one who could "fill in the vacancies in the smaller towns" where the "great lights could not always be secured."

What a glorious galaxy of great names that original list of Redpath lecturers contained! Henry Ward Beecher, John B. Gough, Senator Charles Sumner, Theodore Tilton, Wendell Phillips, Mrs. Mary A. Livermore, Bayard Taylor, Ralph Waldo Emerson, with many of the great preachers, musicians, and writers of that remarkable era. Even Dr. Holmes, John Whittier, Henry W. Longfellow, John Lothrop Motley, George William Curtis, and General Burnside were persuaded to appear one or more times, although they refused to receive pay. I cannot forget how ashamed I felt when my name appeared in the shadow of such names, and how sure I was that every acquaintance was ridiculing me behind my back. Mr. Bayard Taylor, however, wrote me from the *Tribune* office a kind note saying that he was glad to see me "on the road to great usefulness." Governor Clafflin, of Massachusetts, took the time to send me a note of congratulation. General Benjamin F. Butler, however, advised me to "stick to the last" and be a good lawyer.

The work of lecturing was always a task and a duty. I do not feel now that I ever sought to be an entertainer. I am sure I would have been an utter failure but for the feeling that I must preach some gospel truth in my lectures and do at least that much toward that ever-persistent "call of God." When I entered the ministry (1879) I had become so associated with the lecture platform in America and England that I could not feel justified in abandoning so great a field of usefulness.

The experiences of all our successful lecturers are probably nearly alike. The way is not always smooth. But the hard roads, the poor hotels, the late trains, the cold halls, the hot church auditoriums, the overkindness of hospitable committees, and the broken hours of sleep are annoyances one soon forgets; and the hosts of intelligent faces, the messages of thanks, and the effects of the earnings on the lives of young college men can never cease to be a daily joy. God bless them all.

Often have I been asked if I did not, in fifty years of travel in all sorts of conveyances, meet with accidents. It is a marvel to me that no such event ever brought me harm. In a continuous period of over twenty-seven years I delivered about two lectures in every three days, yet I did not miss a single engagement. Sometimes I had to hire a special train, but I reached the town on time, with only a rare exception, and then I was but a few minutes late. Accidents have preceded and followed me on trains and boats, and were sometimes in sight, but I was preserved without injury through all the years. In the Johnstown flood region I saw a bridge go out behind our train. I was once on a derelict steamer on the Atlantic for twenty-six days. At another time a man was killed in the berth of a sleeper I had left half an hour before. Often have I felt the train leave the track, but no one was killed. Robbers have several times threatened my life, but all came out without loss to me. God and man have ever been patient with me.

Yet this period of lecturing has been, after all, a side issue. The Temple, and its church, in Philadelphia, which, when its membership was less than three thousand members, for so many years contributed through its membership over sixty thousand dollars a year for the uplift of humanity, has made life a continual surprise; while the Samaritan Hospital's amazing growth, and the Garretson Hospital's dispensaries, have been so continually ministering to the sick and poor, and have done such skilful work for the tens of thousands who ask for their help each year, that I have been made happy while away lecturing by the feeling that each hour and minute they were faithfully doing good. Temple University, which was founded only twenty-seven years ago, has already sent out into a higher income and nobler life nearly a hundred thousand young men and women who could not probably have obtained an education in any other institution. The faithful, self-sacrificing faculty, now numbering two hundred and fifty-three professors, have done the real work. For that I can claim but little credit; and I mention the University here only to show that my "fifty years on the lecture platform" has necessarily been a side line of work.

My best-known lecture, "Acres of Diamonds," was a mere accidental address, at first given before a reunion of my old comrades of the Forty-sixth Massachusetts Regiment, which served in the Civil War and in which I was captain. I had no thought of giving the address again, and even after it began to be called for by lecture committees I did not dream that I should live to deliver it, as I now have done, almost five thousand times. "What is the secret of its popularity?" I could never explain to myself or others. I simply know that I always attempt to enthuse myself on each occasion with the idea that it is a special opportunity to do good, and I interest myself in each community and apply the general principles with local illustrations.

The hand which now holds this pen must in the natural course of events soon cease to gesture on the platform, and it is a sincere, prayerful hope that this book will go on into the years doing increasing good for the aid of my brothers and sisters in the human family.

Russell H. Conwell.

South Worthington, Mass.,
September 1, 1913.

[1] The life of Henry Ward Beecher parallels that of Russell H. Conwell in many respects. His Plymouth Church in Brooklyn became the largest in America with a seating capacity of nearly 3,000. But it was not to this audience alone that he preached; for, believing as Dean Conwell did after him, that all things concerning the public welfare are fit subjects for a minister's attention, his opinions on all questions were eagerly followed by the public at large. He was, perhaps, the most popular lecturer in the country of his day, and was an unrivaled after-dinner speaker. He allied himself with the Republican party as soon as it was formed, lent his pen and pulpit to further its aims, and during the canvass of 1856 traveled far and wide to speak at mass meetings.

Beecher visited Europe in 1863 for his health and when in Great Britain he addressed vast audiences on the purpose and issues of the Civil War, speaking in one instance for three hours consecutively, and changing materially the state of public opinion. He was a strong advocate of free trade and of woman suffrage. His last public speech was in favor of high license, at Chickering Hall, New York, Feb. 25, 1887.

It was as a speaker that Beecher was seen at his best. His mastery of the English tongue, his dramatic power, his instinctive art of impersonation which had become a second nature, his vivid imagination, his breadth of intellectual view, the catholicity of his sympathies, and his passionate enthusiasm made him a preacher without a peer in his own time and country. Later, like Beecher, Conwell was without peer in his day and the description which characterizes the former applies with equal force to Conwell himself.

[2] Preach on Sunday.

THE END